Recipe Hacks

for

Dry Ranch

Salad Dressing

And Dip Mix

Laura Sommers is **The Recipe Lady!**

She is the #1 Best Selling Author of over 80 recipe books.

She is a loving wife and mother who lives on a small farm in Baltimore County, Maryland and has a passion for all things domestic especially when it comes to saving money. She has a profitable eBay business and is a couponing addict. Follow her tips and tricks to learn how to make delicious meals on a budget, save money or to learn the latest life hack!

Visit her Amazon Author Page to see her latest books:

amazon.com/author/laurasommers

Visit the Recipe Lady's blog for even more great recipes and to learn which books are **FREE** for download each week:

http://the-recipe-lady.blogspot.com/

Subscribe to The Recipe Lady blog through Amazon and have recipes and updates sent directly to your Kindle:

The Recipe Lady Blog through Amazon

Laura Sommers is also an Extreme Couponer and Penny Hauler! If you would like to find out how to get things for **FREE** with coupons or how to get things for only a **PENNY**, then visit her couponing blog **Penny Items and Freebies**

http://penny-items-and-freebies.blogspot.com/

Introduction

Ranch salad dressing is one of the greatest inventions of our time. There, I've said it. And with the addition of the dry ranch ingredients in ready to use one ounce envelope packets, creativity should know no bounds.

The seasoning packets are so versatile for adding flavor to soups, chicken, dips and casseroles. Every pantry should have a supply of ranch salad dressing and dip mix packets ready to go. Here is a cookbook full of mouth-watering and delicious recipes that all use dry ranch salad dressing and dip mix so that your meals and parties are never boring. You will want to try them all. Because ranch dressing mix is a secret weapon every cook can use if they know how to hack it!

Ranch Mashed Potatoes

Ingredients:

2 lbs. peeled Idaho potatoes, chopped
3 tbsps. butter, softened
1/3 cup half-and-half
1 tbsp. chipotle peppers in adobo sauce
2 tbsps. dry ranch salad dressing and dip mix
Salt to taste
Pepper to taste

Directions:

1. Place potatoes in large pan with water over high heat and boil until tender but still firm, about 15-20 minutes.
2. Heat butter, half-and-half and peppers in saucepan over low heat until combined.
3. Drain potatoes and place in mixer with butter sauce.
4. Add dressing mix and process until smooth. Season with salt and pepper.

Ranch Pasta Primavera Salad

Ingredients:

1/2 (1 oz.) envelope dry ranch salad dressing and dip mix
1/2 cup milk
1/2 cup mayonnaise
3 tbsps. olive oil or vegetable oil
2 zucchini, cut into
1/4-inch slices
1 cup frozen broccoli florets, steamed
1 red bell pepper or green bell pepper, cut into small chunks
1 cup cherry tomatoes, halved
4 medium radishes, thinly sliced
3 green onions, chopped
1 (16 oz.) package rotini (corkscrew) pasta
2 tbsps. drained capers (optional)

Directions:

1. Cook pasta according to package directions. Rinse with cool water and drain.
2. Combine dry ranch salad dressing mix with milk and mayonnaise in a bowl, creating 1 cup dressing.
1. In a small bowl, whisk the dressing together with the oil until emulsified.
2. In a large bowl, add the pasta and the remaining ingredients.
3. Add the dressing and toss until well coated.
4. Chill covered for 1 hour before serving.

Ranch Potato Skins

Ingredients:

4 baked potatoes, quartered 1/4 cup sour cream
1 (1 oz.) envelope dry ranch salad dressing and dip mix
1 cup shredded Cheddar cheese
Sliced green onions (optional)
Bacon pieces (optional)

Directions:

1. Scoop the potato out of the skins; combine with sour cream and dressing mix. Fill skins with mixture. Sprinkle with cheese.
2. Bake at 375 degrees F for 12-15 minutes or until cheese is melted.
3. Garnish with green onions and/or bacon bits, if desired.

Ranch Meatloaf

Ingredients:

3/4 pound ground beef
1 egg, beaten
1 (1 oz.) envelope dry ranch salad dressing and dip mix
1/3 cup dry bread crumbs

Directions:

1. Preheat oven to 350 F.
2. Mix all ingredients together in a bowl, but avoid excessive handling for a moist meatloaf.
3. Form into a loaf and place in a baking dish or loaf pan.
4. Bake for 40-45 minutes or until the internal temperature reaches 165 degrees F.
5. Remove from oven and let the meatloaf stand covered for 10-15 minutes before slicing.

Ranch Bacon & Cheddar Dip

Ingredients:

1 (16 oz.) container sour cream
1 (1 oz.) envelope dry ranch salad dressing and dip mix
1 cup shredded Cheddar cheese
6 thick-cut bacon, cooked and crumbled
Freshly cut vegetables, corn or potato chips

Directions:

1. In a bowl, add the sour cream and dips mix and stir until well blended. Fold in the cheese and bacon.
2. Chill covered for 1 hour before serving.

Mississippi Ranch Roast

Ingredients:

1 (3 1/2) pound boneless beef chuck roast Kosher salt and ground black pepper, to taste
1/4 cup flour
3 tbsps. olive oil
1/2 cup beef broth
1 (1 oz.) envelope dry ranch salad dressing and dip mix
1/2 cup butter
8 pepperoncini

Directions:

1. Season chuck roast generously with salt and pepper.
2. Rub flour evenly over the surface of the meat.
3. In a large saute pan, warm oil over high heat until very hot but not smoking. Sear the roast until browned and crusty on all sides, about 15 minutes total.
4. Place roast in the pot of a slow cooker.
5. Pour beef broth around the roast.
6. Sprinkle Ranch seasoning over the roast, place butter on top and scatter pepperoncini over and around the roast.
7. Cover the slow cooker and set on low heat for 7-8 hours.
8. When ready, shred the meat and mix with the sauce in the slow cooker. Serve over bread, egg noodles or potatoes.

Ranch Pork Chops

Ingredients:

1 (1 oz.) envelope dry ranch salad dressing and dip mix
6 pork loin rib chops, about 1 inch thick
1 dash paprika (optional)
Salt to taste
Fresh cracked black pepper to taste

Directions:

1. Preheat the oven to 450 degrees F.
2. In a small bowl, add the seasoning mix, together with the salt, pepper, and paprika and mix well.
3. Liberally sprinkle the pork chops on both sides with the seasoning mixture.
4. Arrange the chops on a baking sheet or try with a rack.
5. Bake the pork chops for 20 minutes, turning once until browned or an internal temperature of 160 degrees F is reached.

Ranch Spinach Dip

Ingredients:

1 (1 oz.) envelope dry ranch salad dressing and dip mix
1 (16 oz.) container sour cream
1 (10 oz.) box frozen chopped spinach, thawed and well drained
1 (8 oz.) can water chestnuts, rinsed, drained and chopped
1 round loaf French bread
Assorted, fresh vegetable sticks cut up for dipping

Directions:

1. Stir together dips mix, sour cream, spinach and water chestnuts.
2. Chill 30 minutes or until just before serving.
3. Cut top off the bread and remove center (using firm bread pieces as dippers).
4. Fill bread bowl with dip. Serve with cubed bread and vegetables.

Ranch Burgers

Ingredients:

1 (1 oz.) envelope dry ranch salad dressing and dip mix
2 pounds lean ground beef
1 small yellow onion, peeled and minced
1 tsp. freshly ground black pepper
1/2 cup seasoned dry bread crumbs (optional)
6 hamburger buns, lightly toasted
6 leaves butter lettuce, or more as needed
1 medium tomato, sliced

Directions:

1. Preheat the grill or broiler.
2. In a large bowl, combine the beef, seasoning mix, onion, and pepper and mix well. If desired, add bread crumbs to meat mixture, too.
3. With wet hands shape the meat mixture into 6 patties, each about 1-inch thick. Grill the burgers for 5 to 7 minutes per side or until an internal temperature of 165 degrees F is reached and juices run clear.
4. Serve the burgers topped with the lettuce and tomato.

Ranch Onion Rings

Ingredients:

1 large yellow onion
1/2 cup flour
2 tsps. dry ranch salad dressing and dip mix
1 cup ranch salad dressing
2 1/2 cups panko bread crumbs
cooking spray

Directions:

1. Preheat oven to 450 degrees F.
2. Line a large baking sheet with parchment paper.
3. Trim ends off onions, peel and cut crosswise into ½ inch slices.
4. Separate onion slices into separate slices.
5. Place flour and seasoning mix in a large resealable plastic bag.
6. Add onion rings and shake in bag until well coated.
7. Pour dressing into a bowl. Put bread crumbs into a separate resealable bag.
8. Individually toss flour-coated onion rings in dressing.
9. Shake off excess before coating with bread crumbs and placing rings on baking sheet.
10. Cover with cooking spray.
11. Bake 15-20 minutes, until golden brown.
12. Option to freeze for 15 minutes before baking for firmer consistency.

Ranch Smashed Potatoes

Ingredients:

2 lbs. Baby Yukon potatoes, rinsed
4 cloves garlic, minced
6 tbsps. butter, melted
1 (1 oz.) envelope dry ranch salad dressing and dip mix
salt and pepper, to taste
garnish with minced parsley (optional)

Directions:

1. Preheat oven to 425 degrees F.
2. Place potatoes in a large pot and cover with water.
3. Add a generous pinch of salt to water, and bring to a boil.
4. Simmer until potatoes are tender (approximately 15-20 minutes), then drain and set aside.
5. Spray a large baking sheet with cooking spray and space potatoes evenly with about an inch of space between them.
6. Then, using a potato masher or large fork, gently press down on each potato until "smashed."
7. Combine garlic and butter in a small bowl, then brush generously on each potato.
8. Sprinkle with seasoning mix, salt and pepper.
9. Bake in preheated oven until potatoes are golden brown and crispy, approximately 25 minutes.
10. Garnish with minced parsley as desired and serve warm.

Ranch Cheese Puff Chicken Tender Lettuce Cups

Ingredients:

2 cups cheese puffs
1 cup kettle-cooked potato chips
1 cup rice flour
1 tbsp. dry ranch salad dressing and dip mix
1 cup whole milk
1 egg
1 lb. chicken tenderloins
4 cups canola oil
Salt to taste
1/2 cup Sriracha sauce
1/4 cup sambal
1 tbsp. lime juice
Bibb lettuce cups (small leaves)
1/2 Serrano chile, sliced thin
cilantro leaves
1/4 cup Greek yogurt
1/2 cup milk
1 tbsp. ranch salad dressing
2 tbsps. dry ranch salad dressing and dip mix

Directions:

1. Crush up the cheese puffs and the potato chips in a food processor until it is ground like coarse breadcrumbs. Place chips in a bowl.
2. In another bowl, mix together the flour and the ranch dressing mix.
3. Set aside.
4. In another bowl, whisk the milk and egg
5. Dredge the chicken in the flour. Dredge in the milk.
6. Then, coat in the chip mix. Press it well to make sure it sticks well.
7. Heat the oil to 350°F. Drop the chicken in the oil and fry in 2 batches. Cook each batch for 3 min. Remove from the oil and drain on a paper towel lined tray. Season with salt.
8. Allow the oil to return to temperature before frying the second batch.
9. In a bowl, mix together Sriracha sauce, sambal and lime juice. Set aside.
10. Place the fried chicken in a lettuce cup. Garnish with hot sauce, chiles and cilantro.
11. Mix remaining ingredients, except seasoning mix, in a bowl.

12. Place into an iSi canister and charge twice.
13. Dispense mixture onto lettuce cups.
14. Sprinkle with dry ranch salad dressing mix.

Ranch Buffalo Wings

Ingredients:

1/2 cup butter or margarine, melted
1/2 tsp. paprika
1/4 cup hot pepper sauce
1 (1 oz.) envelope dry ranch salad dressing and dip mix
24 chicken wings
3 tbsps. vinegar
celery sticks
1 cup ranch salad dressing

Directions:

1. Preheat oven to 350 degrees F.
2. In small bowl, whisk together butter, hot sauce and vinegar.
3. Dip wings in butter mixture; arrange in single layer in large baking pan.
4. Sprinkle with dry ranch salad dressing mix.
5. Bake about 30 to 40 minutes until done.
6. Sprinkle with paprika.
7. Serve with ranch salad dressing and celery sticks.

Ranch Oyster Crackers

Ingredients:

2 1/2 tbsps. freshly chopped dill (or 1 tsp. dried)
1/4 cup vegetable oil
1 16-oz. box oyster crackers
1 (1 oz.) envelope dry ranch salad dressing and dip mix
1/4 tsp. lemon pepper, and/or garlic powder

Directions:

1. Preheat the oven to 250 degrees F.
2. In a small bowl, add the oil, ranch salad dressing mix, dill, and lemon pepper and/or garlic powder. Stir until mixed through.
3. In a 1-gallon-size Glad® Zipper Bag, add the crackers and oil mixture.
4. Seal the bag and toss until well-coated.
5. Arrange the crackers on an ungreased half-sheet pan in a single layer.
6. Bake the crackers for 15 to 20 minutes or until golden.

Ranch Drummies

Ingredients:

1/2 cup butter
1/2 cup mayonnaise
1/2 cup sour cream
3/4 cup flour
1 (1 oz.) envelope dry ranch salad dressing and dip mix
1 (1 oz.) envelope dry buttermilk ranch salad dressing and dip mix
1 tsp. hot pepper sauce or more if needed
2 tsps. cracked black pepper
3 pounds chicken drummies
Crudité, such as carrots, celery, bell pepper

Hot Pepper Ranch Directions:

1. Stir together 2 1/2 tbsps. buttermilk ranch mix, mayonnaise, sour cream and hot pepper sauce.
2. Refrigerate until ready to serve.

Drummies Directions:

1. Rinse drummies and pat dry with paper towels.
2. Sprinkle all sides of drummies with garlic pepper; set aside.
3. Combine ranch dressing mix with flour in large ziptop bag.
4. Add drummies and shake until coated.
5. Place butter on a rimmed baking sheet.
6. Place in oven until butter has melted and begins to sizzle.
7. Add drummies to sheet and bake for 20 minutes.
8. Turn and continue baking for another 20 minutes, or until golden brown.
9. Serve drummies with crudités and hot pepper ranch for dipping.

Ranch Twice Baked Potatoes

Ingredients:

4 large baking potatoes
1 tbsp. dry buttermilk ranch salad dressing and dip mix
1/2 cup sour cream
4 tbsps. butter softened
1/2 tsp. garlic minced
1/8 to 1/4 tsp. black pepper
3/4 cup grated cheese divided into 1/2 cup portion and 1/4 cup portion
2 green onions chopped
paprika for garnish
bacon bits
3/4 cup buttermilk
Ranch salad dressing

Directions:

1. Preheat oven to 350 degrees F.
2. Pierce potatoes 6-8 times with a fork.
3. Place pierced potatoes, not touching, on a large baking sheet.
4. Bake potatoes in a 350°F oven for 1 to 1 ½ hours until done.
5. Let them cool 10–15 minutes.
6. Slice potatoes in half lengthwise. Using a spoon, carefully scoop out flesh leaving ¼-inch of potato on the skin so they don't break.
7. Place potato skins on baking sheet and set aside.
8. In a large bowl blend the following ingredients until well blended and creamy.
9. Taste and adjust seasonings, if necessary.
10. Top with remaining ¼ cup cheese, green onions and bacon bits.
11. Lightly sprinkle with paprika.
12. Return to oven until hot and cheese is melted, about 15–20 minutes.
13. Top with ranch salad dressing.

Ranch Holiday Ham

Ingredients:

3/4 cup honey
1 (3-5 pounds) whole, bone-in, smoked ham
1 (1 oz.) envelope dry ranch salad dressing and dip mix
2 tbsps. apple cider vinegar
2 tsps. whole cloves
3 tbsps. mustard

Directions:

1. Preheat oven to 325 degrees F.
2. In a saucepan over a medium low heat, combine the honey, vinegar, and dressing mix and stir until well blended.
3. Stud the top of the ham with whole cloves.
4. Drizzle the sauce over the ham and bake for 20 minutes per pound or until the sauce turns to a glaze and an internal temperature of 140 degrees F is reached.

Ranch Holiday Turkey

Ingredients:

1/2 cup unsalted butter at room temperature
1 12-14 pound turkey giblets and liver removed, rinsed well, patted dry
2 (1 oz.) envelope dry ranch salad dressing and dip mix

Directions:

1. Preheat the oven to 350 degrees F.
2. In a small bowl, mix the butter together with one of the packets of seasoning mix until well blended.
3. With clean hands, carefully separate the breast skin from the breast by moving your hand underneath the skin.
4. Spread the butter mixture evenly under the skin.
5. Sprinkle the remaing packet of seasoning mix all over the turkey.
6. Roast the turkey covered for 3 hours, then uncover and cook for another 30 minutes or until juices run clear and an internal temperature of 165 degrees F is reached.

Ranch Pineapple Chicken Sticks

Ingredients:

2 1/2 cups pineapple juice
2 (1 oz.) envelope dry ranch salad dressing and dip mix
4 chicken breast halves, skinned, (1 pound), boned
2 tsps. cornstarch
2 tbsps. water

Directions:

1. Whisk juice and dressing mix together.
2. Reserve half.
3. Cut chicken into 16 long strips.
4. Marinate strips in remaining juice mixture, 2–24 hours.
5. Thread on skewers.
6. Grill/broil to desired doneness.
7. Combine cornstarch, water and reserved mixture in saucepan.
8. Heat to thicken.
9. Dip chicken in sauce to serve.
10. To microwave skewers, microwave chicken on high, covered, 6–8 minutes per pound.
11. Let stand 5 minutes before serving.

Pumpkin Spice Empanadas

Ingredients:

1 package (2 9-in. crusts) refrigerated pie crusts
1 cup canned pumpkin pulp, NOT pumpkin pie filling
1 egg, plus additional egg for brushing the top
1 1/2 tsps. dry ranch salad dressing and dip mix

Directions:

1. Preheat oven to 400°F. Line a rimmed baking sheet with parchment paper.
2. Unroll each pie crust onto a lightly floured surface and cut out circles using a 3–3½-inch cookie cutter. You will get 7–8.
3. Lay rounds on a flat surface.
4. In a small bowl mix together the pumpkin puree, seasoning mix and egg until well blended.
5. Spoon about 2 tsps. of the mixture into the center of each round, making sure you leave the border around the filling clean.
6. Dip your finger in water and run it around the clean edge of the pie dough. Gently fold the empanadas in half.
7. Using the tines of a fork, press down on the edges to seal them.
8. In a small bowl, whisk together another egg with water.
9. Using a pastry brush, lightly brush the tops of the empanadas with egg mixture. Bake for about 20 minutes or until golden brown.
10. Serve with ranch salad dressing, for dipping.

Spicy Ranch Roasted Chickpeas

Ingredients:

1 16-oz. can garbanzo beans, rinsed and dried with paper towels
1 tbsp. extra-virgin olive oil, plus more for coating the pan
1 tbsp. dry ranch salad dressing and dip mix

Directions:

1. Preheat oven to 425 degrees F.
2. Line a rimmed baking sheet with foil and coat lightly with oil.
3. In a medium bowl, toss together garbanzo beans, olive oil and 1 tbsp. of the seasoning mix.
4. Pour onto prepared baking sheet and sprinkle with remaining seasoning.
5. Bake for 15 minutes, stir, and bake an additional 10 minutes or until golden and slightly crispy.

Buffalo Ranch Popcorn

Ingredients:

8 cups popped popcorn
1 tsp. dry ranch salad dressing and dip mix
2 tbsps. buffalo wing sauce
2 tbsps. melted butter

Directions:

1. Place popped popcorn in a large bowl.
2. Sprinkle with ranch dressing dry seasoning and toss to coat.
3. Combine melted butter and wing sauce and stir well.
4. Pour over popcorn and toss to coat.

Parmesan-Ranch Oven Fries

Ingredients:

2-3 tbsps. olive oil
6-8 new potatoes
1 egg, well beaten
1 (1 oz.) envelope dry ranch salad dressing and dip mix
3 tbsps. cornstarch
1/2 cup shredded parmesan
Pepper

Directions:

1. Clean potatoes, slicing them into thin spears.
2. Transfer them to a large bowl and pour the beaten egg over the potatoes.
3. Stir together until they are all shiny from the egg.
4. Sprinkle with cornstarch, parmesan, and about 1/2 the packet of ranch dressing mix.
5. Use more or less, depending on your desired level of saltiness.
6. Stir gently to spread the coating fairly evenly throughout the potatoes.
7. Turn potatoes onto a lightly greased cookie sheet.
8. Bake in an oven preheated to 425 degrees for 20 minutes.
9. Using a large spatula, flip the potatoes to the other side and return to oven for an additional 20-25 minutes, or until crisp and browned.

Crock Pot Ranch Pork Chops

Ingredients:

6 pork chops, 1/2 inch thick
1 (1 oz.) envelope dry ranch salad dressing and dip mix
1 10-oz. can cream of chicken soup

Directions:

1. Place pork chops, ranch seasoning and soup into a Crock pot.
2. Cook on high heat for 4 hours or low heat for 6 hours.
3. Serve with mashed potatoes.

Cheddar Bacon Ranch Pull Apart Bread

Ingredients:

1 1 pound loaf sour dough bread
1/2 cup melted butter
1 tbsp. dry ranch salad dressing and dip mix
6 oz. cheddar cheese sliced thin
4 oz. of bacon

Directions:

1. Preheat oven to 425 degrees.
2. Place bacon on a foil lined cookie sheet, and bake bacon for 8 to 10 minutes.
3. Reset the temperature of the oven to 350 degrees.
4. The bacon will be undercooked. Once bacon cools slightly slice bacon into small pieces.
5. In a small pot melt 1/2 cup of butter, and add 1 tbsp. dry Ranch dressing mix, stir to combine well.
6. Slice bread diagonally about 1 inch slices, do not slice into bread completely, leave a good one inch that is not sliced completely.
7. Rotate bread 90 degrees and slide again, in one inch slices.
8. Push cheese slices into sliced bread.
9. Place bacon slices into sliced bread.
10. Drizzle butter and Ranch dressing mix mixture over the bread.
11. Wrap the bread in foil, and bake for about 10-15 minutes at 350 degrees, and then unwrap the top of the bread and bake for an additional 10-15 minutes.

Crudite Pizza

Ingredients:

1/2 (1 oz.) envelope dry ranch salad dressing and dip mix or to taste
1/2 cup sour cream
2 tbsps. mayonnaise
1 (8 oz.) package cream cheese, softened
2 (8 oz.) cans crescent rolls
Vegetables, carrots, bell peppers, cucumber, etc., sliced

Directions:

1. Combine the dry ranch dressing mix with the sour cream.
2. Add the mayo and cream; stir well. Refrigerate at least one hour, preferably overnight.
3. Lay the sheets of crescent roll dough into a half sheet pan and press to completely cover the bottom of the pan.
4. Bake according to the package directions. Allow to cool, leaving the bread crust in the pan.
5. Stir the refrigerated ranch spread to loosen, thinning with a little milk, if necessary and spread over the crust.
6. Cut the pizza into small serving sizes, then refrigerate the pan until ready to serve.

Ranch Taco Soup

Ingredients:

1 pound lean ground beef
1 pound pork breakfast sausage
2 cans Rotel tomatoes
2 cans pinto beans, undrained
3 cups water
1 can mexi-corn, undrained
1 (1 oz.) envelope dry ranch salad dressing and dip mix
1 package taco seasoning

Directions:

1. Brown and drain beef and pork in large stew pot.
2. Add remaining ingredients and cook on medium-low heat for 30 minutes.
3. An alternate method is to brown meats and pour meats and all remaining ingredients into a large crock pot or slow cooker and cook on low for 4 to 6 hours.
4. Garnish soup with chopped green onions, sour cream, shredded cheddar cheese, and Tortilla Chips.

Fried Pickle Ranch Burgers

Fried Pickles Ingredients:

12 dill pickle slices
1 cup milk
1 egg
1 cup flour
2 tbsps. dry ranch dressing mix
1/2 tsp. salt
1/4 tsp. black pepper
Canola oil for frying

Burger Ingredients:

4 hamburger patties
1 tbsp. dry ranch salad dressing and dip mix
Salt and pepper to taste
Worcestershire sauce
1 cup shredded cheddar cheese, divided
4 buns, toasted
Ranch dressing

Pickles Directions:

1. Heat about an inch of canola oil in a large skillet over medium-high heat. Combine milk and egg.
2. Combine flour, ranch mix, salt and pepper.
3. Dip the pickle slices first in the milk mixture, then in the flour mixture.
4. Dip in the milk mixture again, then in the flour mixture again.
5. Fry pickles in batches until coating is browned and crisp.
6. Remove to paper towels and sprinkle with salt.

Burgers Directions:

1. Season each patty with ranch mix and salt and pepper.
2. Cook in a skillet to desired doneness; drizzle with some Worcestershire.
3. Top each burger with 1/4 cup shredded cheddar cheese and cover the skillet until the cheese is melted.
4. To assemble the burgers, top the bottom half of each bun with a burger patty and 3 fried pickles.
5. Slather the top of each bun with ranch dressing and serve.

Ranch BLT Pasta Salad

Ingredients:

1/2 cup mayonnaise
1 tbsp. dry ranch salad dressing and dip mix
1 tbsp. olive oil
1 large leek, cleaned and sliced (bottom white part only
1-2 medium tomatoes, seeded and diced
1/2 cup crumbled cooked bacon
1/2 cup shredded cheddar or Monterey jack cheese
12 oz. your favorite shape, cooked al dente

Directions:

1. Mix together the mayonnaise and dry ranch dressing mix in the bottom of a large bowl, set aside.
2. In a medium skillet over medium high heat, add the oil and saute the chopped leeks. Cook until softened.
3. Add the leeks to the large bowl along with the remaining ingredients.
4. Carefully fold in all the ingredients to incorporate and coat with the ranch dressing.
5. Season with salt and pepper to taste.
6. Cover with plastic wrap and chill for at least an hour before serving to allow time for

Chaddar Ranch Chicken

Ingredients:

4 boneless skinless chicken breasts
1/2 cup mayonnaise
2 tbsps. dry ranch salad dressing and dip mix
1/4 cup grated cheddar cheese
1/4 cup panko bread crumbs
cooking spray

Directions:

1. Preheat the oven to 425 degrees.
2. Place the chicken in a large baking dish.
3. In a small bowl, combine the mayonnaise, ranch, and cheddar cheese.
4. Spread on top of the chicken breasts.
5. Sprinkle the panko on top and spray lightly with cooking spray.
6. Bake for 25 minutes or until chicken is cooked through.

Bacon Ranch Cheese Ball

Ingredients:

2 (8 oz each) packages cream cheese
1 (1 oz.) envelope dry buttermilk ranch salad dressing and dip mix
1/2 cup cheddar cheese, grated
1/4 cup green onion, thinly sliced
6 pieces of bacon, fried and crumbled
¼ cup chopped black olives, optional
1 cup pecans or almonds, finely chopped for coating

Directions:

1. Mix together the cream cheese and dry ranch packet until smooth.
2. Add the cheese, onions, olive if using and bacon.
3. Shape into a ball.
4. Roll it in the nuts to coat the outside.
5. Store in the refrigerator.

Cheesy Bacon Ranch Potato Soup

Ingredients:

3/4 cup sour cream
1/4 cup mayonnaise
1/4 cup whole milk
1 1/2 tbsp. dry ranch salad dressing and dip mix
3 lbs. Russet potatoes peeled and diced into 1" cubes
1 tbsp. extra virgin olive oil
3/4 cup diced yellow onion (about 1 small onion)
2 cloves garlic finely minced
2 (14.5 oz.) cans chicken broth*
2 cups whole milk
1/4 cup all-purpose flour
1 1/2 cups sharp cheddar cheese divided
1/4 cup finely grated Parmesan cheese
Freshly ground black pepper to taste
10 slices bacon cooked and crumbled
3 green onions chopped

Directions:

1. In a mixing bowl, whisk together sour cream, mayonnaise, 1/4 cup milk and ranch seasoning mix. Cover bowl and refrigerate.
2. Heat olive oil a large cast iron dutch oven over medium high heat. Add onion and saute about 4 minutes until golden, add garlic and saute 1 more minute.
3. Add chicken broth and diced potatoes and bring mixture just to a boil, then reduce heat to medium, cover pot and cook 15 - 20 minutes until potatoes are very tender.
4. In a mixing bowl, whisk together 2 cups milk with 1/4 cup flour and pour mixture into soup.
5. Increase temperature to medium high heat, and bring mixture just to a boil, stirring constantly.
6. Once mixture reaches a boil, reduce heat to low, add ranch dressing mixture from refrigerator, 1 cup (4 oz.) grated Cheddar cheese, grated Parmesan cheese and season with black pepper to taste.
7. Cook about 5 minutes, stirring frequently.
8. Serve warm, sprinkle each serving with remaining cheddar cheese, bacon, and green onions.

Ranch Fries

Ingredients:

3 large potatoes, scrubbed
1 cup milk
1 (1 oz.) envelope dry ranch salad dressing and dip mix
1 pinch garlic salt 1 quart oil for frying, or as needed

Directions:

1. Heat oil in a deep-fryer to 365 degrees F (185 degrees C).
2. Cut potatoes into wedges or fries, and soak in a bowl with milk.
3. Stir together the ranch dressing mix and garlic salt; place on a plate or in a bag.
4. Drain potatoes, and roll in the seasonings to coat.
5. Place potatoes into the deep-fryer in batches so they are not too crowded. Fry for 5 minutes, or until golden brown.
6. Drain on paper towels, and season with leftover seasoning mixture.

Ranch Baked Potatoes and Vegetables

Ingredients:

1/2 cup olive oil
1 (1 oz.) envelope dry ranch salad dressing and dip mix
4 large potatoes, peeled and coarsely chopped
2 zucchini, coarsely chopped
3 stalks celery, coarsely chopped, or more to taste
1 onion, coarsely chopped, optional
1/2 cup seasoned bread crumbs
1 pinch garlic salt

Directions:

1. Preheat oven to 350 degrees F (175 degrees C).
2. Mix olive oil and ranch dressing mix together in an 8-inch square baking pan. Add 1/2 of the potatoes, 1/2 of the zucchini, 1/2 of the onion, and 1/2 of the onion; stir to coat.
3. Add remaining potatoes, zucchini, celery, and onion; stir to coat. Sprinkle bread crumbs and garlic salt over the top.
4. Bake in the preheated oven until vegetables are tender, 50 to 60 minutes.

Chipotle Ranch Dip

Ingredients:

1 cup mayonnaise 1 cup light sour cream
2 1/2 tbsps. dry ranch dressing mix
3 green onions, minced
1 clove garlic, minced
1 tbsp. fresh lime juice
1 canned chipotle chile in adobo sauce, minced, or more to taste

Directions:

1. Whisk the mayonnaise, sour cream, ranch dressing mix, green onions, garlic, lime juice, and chipotle chile together in a bowl until blended.
2. Serve immediately, or refrigerate until needed.

Ranch Party Dip

Ingredients:

2 (1 oz.) envelope dry ranch salad dressing and dip mix
1 (16 oz.) jar mayonnaise
1 (16 oz.) container sour cream
1 (8 oz.) container cottage cheese
1 tbsp. lemon juice
1 tsp. garlic salt 1 tsp. onion powder
1 1/2 tsps. ground cayenne pepper

Directions:

1. In a large bowl, mix together dry ranch-style dressing mix, mayonnaise, sour cream, cottage cheese, lemon juice, garlic salt, onion powder and cayenne pepper.
2. Chill in the refrigerator until serving.

Spicy Buffalo Party Mix

Ingredients:

1/2 cup butter
1/2 cup hot sauce
 1 (1 oz.) envelope dry ranch salad dressing and dip mix
6 cups crispy rice cereal squares
4 cups crispy wheat cereal squares
1 3/4 cups dry-roasted peanuts
1 1/2 cups fish-shaped pretzel
1 1/2 cups Parmesan-flavored fish-shaped crackers

Directions:

1. Preheat oven to 350 degrees F (175 degrees C).
2. Heat butter in a microwave-safe bowl in the microwave until melted, 25 to 30 seconds. Add hot sauce and microwave until heated through, 20 to 30 seconds more. Stir in ranch seasoning.
3. Combine rice cereal squares, wheat cereal squares, peanuts, pretzel crackers, and Parmesan-flavored crackers in a large bowl.
4. Pour in butter mixture; mix thoroughly to coat. Spread in 2 ungreased 9x13-inch baking pans.
5. Bake in the preheated oven until golden, about 15 minutes.
6. Remove from oven and stir well. Return to the oven; bake until dried, about 15 minutes more. Spread on paper towels to cool.

Ranch Pretzels

Ingredients:

1 (15 oz.) package pretzels
3/4 cup olive oil
1 (1 oz.) envelope dry ranch salad dressing and dip mix
3 tbsps. garlic powder 3 tbsps. dried dill weed

Directions:

1. Break the pretzels into a large bowl.
2. In a medium bowl, blend the olive oil, ranch salad dressing mix, garlic powder and dill weed.
3. Pour the mixture over the pretzels.
4. Marinate 1 hour, tossing approximately every 10 minutes.
5. Preheat oven to 350 degrees F (175 degrees C).
6. Spread the marinated pretzels on a large cookie sheet.
7. Bake approximately 10 minutes. Allow the pretzels to cool, then serve.

Creamy Jalapeno Dip

Ingredients:

2 whole fresh jalapeno peppers, seeded, deveined and minced
1 (16 oz.) container sour cream
1 (1 oz.) envelope dry ranch salad dressing and dip mix
1 tbsp. garlic powder
2 tbsps. chopped fresh cilantro

Directions:

1. Place minced jalapenos, sour cream, ranch dressing mix, garlic powder, and cilantro in a blender or food processor.
2. Blend until smooth.
3. Cover and refrigerate at least one hour, or overnight, before serving.

Spicy Ranch Cajun Pretzels

Ingredients:

1 (16 oz.) package mini sourdough pretzels
1 cup corn oil
1 (1 oz.) envelope dry ranch salad dressing and dip mix
1 tbsp. Cajun seasoning
1 tsp. cayenne pepper
1 tsp. dried dill weed

Directions:

1. Preheat oven to 200 degrees F.
2. Place broken pretzels in a large baking pan or roaster.
3. Combine corn oil, ranch dressing mix, Cajun seasoning, cayenne pepper and dill.
4. Pour over pretzels; stir to coat evenly.
5. Bake for 2 hours, stirring every 30 minutes.
6. Remove from oven and drain on paper towels to absorb excess oil. Store in tightly covered container.

Ranch Squash

Ingredients:

2 tbsps. butter
3 pounds yellow squash, chopped
2 onions, chopped
1 cup shredded sharp Cheddar cheese
1 cup mayonnaise
3 eggs, beaten
12 saltine crackers, crushed
1 (1 oz.) envelope dry ranch salad dressing and dip mix
1 tsp. salt
2 cups dry bread stuffing mix
1/2 cup melted butter

Directions:

1. Preheat oven to 350 degrees F (175 degrees C).
2. Melt 2 tbsps. butter in a large saucepan over medium-high heat.
3. Cook squash and onions until tender.
4. Remove from heat, and stir in Cheddar cheese, mayonnaise, eggs, and crackers. Season with Ranch dressing mix and salt.
5. Spread the squash mixture into a medium baking dish.
6. Mix together stuffing and 1/2 cup melted butter, and sprinkle over the squash mixture.
7. Bake 20 to 30 minutes in the preheated oven, or until firm and lightly browned.

Buffalo Ranch Chicken Wings

Ingredients:

1 gallon oil for frying, or as needed
3 pounds chicken wings and drummies
1/2 cup unsalted butter
1 (12 fluid oz.) can or bottle hot pepper sauce
1 (1 oz.) envelope dry ranch salad dressing and dip mix
1 tbsp. white vinegar

Directions:

1. Heat oil in a deep-fryer or large saucepan to 375 degrees F (190 degrees C).
2. Fry chicken wings in small batches in hot oil until no longer pink at the bone and the juices run clear, about 15 minutes per batch.
3. An instant-read thermometer inserted into the thickest part of the thigh, near the bone should read 165 degrees F (74 degrees C).
4. Melt butter in a saucepan over low heat. Stir hot sauce, ranch dressing mix, and vinegar into the melted butter.
5. Put cooked chicken wings in a large mixing bowl.
6. Ladle sauce over wings and toss to coat.

Ranch Cauliflower

Ingredients:

1 head cauliflower
1/2 cup sour cream
1/2 cup shredded Cheddar cheese
1 tsp. dry ranch salad dressing mix
1/2 tsp. onion powder
1/2 tsp. garlic powder
1 tbsp. butter, cut into small pieces, or more to taste

Directions:

1. Preheat oven to 350 degrees F (175 degrees C).
2. Place a steamer insert into a saucepan and fill with water to just below the bottom of the steamer.
3. Bring water to a boil.
4. Add cauliflower, cover, and steam until very tender, 15 to 20 minutes. Transfer cauliflower to a bowl, mash, and strain excess water.
5. Mix cauliflower, sour cream, Cheddar cheese, ranch dressing mix, onion powder, and garlic powder together in a 9-inch baking dish; top with butter.
6. Bake in the preheated oven until bubbling, 30 to 45 minutes.

Jalapeno Ranch Bites

Ingredients:

1 (8 oz.) package cream cheese, softened
1 cup shredded Cheddar cheese
1/4 cup mayonnaise
1 (1 oz.) envelope dry ranch salad dressing and dip mix
1 1/2 tsps. garlic powder
20 large jalapeno peppers, halved and seeded
1 pound sliced bacon, cut in half

Directions:

1. Preheat an oven to 400 degrees F (200 degrees C).
2. Stir together the cream cheese, Cheddar cheese, mayonnaise, ranch dressing mix, and garlic powder in a mixing bowl until evenly blended.
3. Spoon some of the cheese mixture into each jalapeno half, wrap with half a bacon strip, and secure with a toothpick.
4. Arrange the wrapped jalapeno halves onto a broiler pan.
5. Bake in the preheated oven until the bacon is no longer pink and beginning to brown, about 20 minutes.

Creamy Cilantro Lime Ranch Dressing

Ingredients:

1 cup buttermilk 1 cup mayonnaise
1/3 bunch fresh cilantro, or to taste
1 fresh tomatillo, husk removed, or more to taste
1/2 lime, juiced
1/2 jalapeno pepper, stemmed and seeded, or more to taste
1 (1 oz.) envelope dry ranch salad dressing and dip mix
1 clove garlic, peeled
1/8 tsp. freshly ground black pepper, or more to taste

Directions:

1. Blend buttermilk, mayonnaise, cilantro, tomatillo, lime juice, jalapeno pepper, ranch dressing mix, garlic, and black pepper together in a blender until smooth.
2. Refrigerate until flavors blend, at least 1 hour.

Ranch Buttermilk Herb Bread

Ingredients:

2 (.25 oz.) envelopes active dry yeast
1/2 cup warm water
1 1/2 cups warm buttermilk (105 to 115 degrees F/43 to 46 degrees C)
1 egg
2 tbsps. vegetable oil
1 (1 oz.) envelope dry ranch salad dressing and dip mix
5 cups all-purpose flour
1 tsp. salt

Directions:

1. In a large bowl, sprinkle the yeast over the warm water. Let stand for about 10 minutes, until foamy.
2. Stir the buttermilk, egg, oil, dressing mix, and salt into the yeast mixture. Stir in 2 cups of the flour using a wooden spoon.
3. Add remaining flour 1/2 cup at a time until the dough can be picked up out of the bowl. Knead on a floured surface for 6 to 8 minutes, until smooth and elastic.
4. Try not to add much more flour.
5. Place in a greased bowl, and turn to coat.
6. Cover with a cloth, and let it rise in a warm place until doubled in size.
7. Press the air out of the dough, and divide into two pieces.
8. Form into tight loaves, and place each one into a greased 8x4 inch loaf pan.
9. Let rise until a your finger leaves a mark when lightly pressed into the dough.
10. Preheat the oven to 350 degrees F (175 degrees C).
11. Bake loaves for about 20 minutes in the preheated oven, until golden brown. When finished, the loaves should sound hollow when tapped on the bottom.

Creamy Apple Slaw

Ingredients:

3/4 cup sour cream
1/3 cup white sugar
3 tbsps. apple cider vinegar
2 tbsps. dry ranch salad dressing and dip mix
1 (8 oz.) package shredded cabbage and carrot mix
3 apples - peeled, cored, and diced
2 stalks celery, chopped
3 green onions, thinly sliced
Salt and ground black pepper to taste

Directions:

1. Whisk sour cream, sugar, vinegar, and ranch dressing mix together in a large bowl; fold in cabbage mix, apples, celery, and green onion.
2. Toss mixture to coat; season with salt and pepper.
3. Cover bowl tightly with plastic wrap and chill until flavors blend, 20 minutes to 4 hours.

Dr. Pepper Ranch Meatballs

Ingredients:

1 1/2 pounds lean ground turkey
1 egg
1 1/4 cups dry bread crumbs
1 (1 oz.) envelope dry ranch salad dressing and dip mix
1 tbsp. Worcestershire sauce
1 onion, minced
1 green bell pepper, minced
1 (12 fl. oz.) can Dr. Pepper® cola
1 tbsp. Worcestershire sauce
1 cup ketchup
1 cup diced tomatoes in juice
1 tsp. salt
1/2 tsp. ground black pepper
1/2 tsp. garlic powder

Directions:

1. Preheat an oven to 375 degrees F (190 degrees C).
2. Place the turkey, egg, bread crumbs, ranch dressing mix, and 1 tbsp. of the Worcestershire sauce into a mixing bowl along with 3 tbsps. of the minced onion, and 3 tbsps. of the minced bell pepper.
3. Set the remaining onion and bell pepper aside.
4. Form the turkey mixture into 2 inch meatballs, and place into a 9x13 inch baking dish.
5. Bake uncovered in the preheated oven for 15 minutes.
6. While the meatballs are baking, stir the remaining onion and bell pepper in a bowl along with the Dr. Pepper(R), 1 tbsp. Worcestershire sauce, ketchup, diced tomatoes, salt, black pepper, and garlic powder.
7. Once the meatballs have cooked for 15 minutes, remove them from the oven and pour the sauce over top.
8. Cover the dish with aluminum foil and return to the oven.
9. Bake for 30 minutes, then remove the foil and continue baking 15 minutes more.
10. Remove from the oven and allow to stand 15 minutes before serving.

Ranch Salmon Patties

Ingredients:

4 pounds pink salmon, drained, flaked
4 large eggs
1 1/2 cups panko bread crumbs
3/4 cup mayonnaise
2 lemons, juiced
2 tbsps. dry ranch salad dressing and dip mix
1 tsp. salt
1 tsp. ground black pepper
1 tsp. garlic powder
1 tsp. dried dill
1 tsp. seafood seasoning (such as Old Bay®)
1/2 cup white cornmeal
1/4 cup vegetable oil, or as needed
16 lemon slices
16 sprigs fresh parsley

Directions:

1. Mix salmon, eggs, bread crumbs, mayonnaise, lemon juice, ranch dressing mix, salt, pepper, garlic powder, dill, and seafood seasoning in a large bowl.
2. Divide into 15 portions and shape into patties.
3. Dust each patty with cornmeal.
4. Heat 1 tbsp. oil in a large skillet. Fry a few patties in hot oil, not overcrowding the skillet, until browned, 3 to 4 minutes per side.
5. Repeat until all patties are cooked.
6. Garnish each with a lemon slice and a sprig of parsley.

Creamy Ranch Cucumber Salad

Ingredients:

4 large cucumbers, sliced
Salt and ground black pepper to taste
1/2 cup half-and-half
1/2 cup sour cream
1/2 cup mayonnaise
5 large green onions, thinly sliced
1 (1 oz.) envelope dry ranch salad dressing and dip mix
1 1/2 tbsps. white sugar
1 tbsp. dried dill weed
1 tsp. celery salt
2 tsps. lime juice

Directions:

1. Arrange cucumber slices in a large bowl, generously seasoning each layer of cucumber with salt and pepper. Cover bowl with plastic wrap and refrigerate for 3 hours.
2. Drain liquid from cucumbers. Gently press cucumber slices with paper towel to absorb any remaining liquid.
3. Stir half-and-half, sour cream, mayonnaise, green onions, ranch dressing mix, sugar, dill, celery salt, and lime juice together in a small bowl; pour over cucumber slices and gently stir to coat.

Traditional Ranch Dip

Ingredients:

1 (1 oz.) envelope dry ranch salad dressing and dip mix
1 (16 oz.) container sour cream

Directions:

1. In a medium bowl, blend all ingredients.
2. Chill if desired.
3. Serve with your favorite dippers.

Oven Roasted Ranch Vegetables

Ingredients:

1 (1 oz.) envelope dry ranch salad dressing and dip mix
1 1/2 pounds assorted fresh vegetables (sliced, zucchini, yellow squash, bell peppers, carrots, celery, onion or mushrooms)

Directions:

1. Preheat oven to 450 degrees F.
2. In a 13x9 inch baking or roasting pan, combine all ingredients until evenly coated.
3. Bake, uncovered, stirring once, for 20 minutes or until vegetables are tender.

Pastrami Ranch Potato Latkes

Ingredients:

2 Yukon gold potatoes
1 egg, lightly beaten
1/2 cup diced pastrami
2 scallions, finely chopped
1 (1 oz.) envelope dry ranch salad dressing and dip mix
1 tbsp. flour
Canola oil, for frying
1/4 cup sour cream
1/4 cup mayonnaise
1/2 cup pastrami for garnish
Chives for garnish

Directions:

1. Peel and grate potatoes.
2. Squeeze out any excess moisture with a clean kitchen towel or paper towels.
3. Combine the potatoes with egg, pastrami, 2 scallions, 1 tbsp. ranch mix and flour.
4. Pour 1 inch of oil in a heavy bottom frying pan and heat on medium high heat, until oil is sizzling.
5. Form tbsp.-sized latkes from mix and fry until golden brown on both sides.
6. Drain on paper towels
7. Combine the remaining ranch dressing, sour cream and mayonnaise.
8. Fry up the pastrami for three minutes.
9. Drain on paper towels and use for garnish.

Ranch Pasta Salad

Ingredients:

1 (12 oz.) box Cavatappi pasta
1 small tomato diced
1 cup fresh broccoli florets cut into bite size pieces
1/4 cup diced yellow pepper
1/4 cup diced orange pepper
salt and pepper to taste
1 cup buttermilk
1 cup mayonnaise
1 (1 oz.) envelope dry ranch salad dressing and dip mix

Directions:

1. Cook pasta al dente.
2. Mix buttermilk and mayo with dry ranch salad dressing mix and set aside.
3. Dice peppers and chop broccoli and tomatoes into bite size pieces.
4. Pour dressing mix over rinsed and cooled pasta.
5. Mix in veggies and stir.
6. Salt and pepper to taste.
7. Refrigerate 2 hours or over-night before serving.

Chicken and Ranch Guacamole

Ingredients:

4 (8-inch) pita bread rounds
1 (1 oz.) envelope dry ranch salad dressing and dip mix
3 tbsps. extra virgin olive oil
2 tsps. hot sauce, such as TABASCO®
1 (12 oz.) fresh prepared guacamole
1 cup thinly sliced kale leaves
1 cup sour cream
1 cup cooked chicken chopped
6 strips cooked bacon broken into bite-sized pieces
1 tbsp. finely chopped, fresh cilantro leaves
Finely grated zest and juice from ½ lime
1 tsp. freshly grated black pepper

Directions:

1. Heat oven to 350 degrees F.
2. Separate each pita bread round to yield 2 thin rounds from each.
3. Stack the rounds, cut in half, and cut each half into fourths to form triangular wedges.
4. Spread the wedges smooth side down on a large baking sheet.
5. Whisk together 1 tbsp. dry ranch mix, 1 tbsp. hot sauce and 2 tbsps. olive oil.
6. Brush mixture on the pita pieces and bake 8 to 10 minutes or until golden brown. Flip the chips so the smooth side is up and bake 5 minutes longer or until brown and crispy.
7. In a serving bowl, mix together the guacamole, kale, sour cream, chicken, bacon, cilantro, lime zest and juice, black pepper, and remaining ranch seasoning mix, remaining 1 tbsp. hot sauce and remaining 1 tbsp. olive oil until combined.
8. Serve dip with warm pita chips.

Traditional Ranch Salad Dressing

Ingredients:

1 (1 oz.) envelope dry ranch salad dressing and dip mix
1 cup buttermilk
1 cup mayonnaise

Directions:

1. Combine all ingredients and stir well.
2. Chill 30 minutes to thicken.
3. Serve and enjoy.

About the Author

Laura Sommers is **The Recipe Lady!**

She is the #1 Best Selling Author of over 80 recipe books.

She is a loving wife and mother who lives on a small farm in Baltimore County, Maryland and has a passion for all things domestic especially when it comes to saving money. She has a profitable eBay business and is a couponing addict. Follow her tips and tricks to learn how to make delicious meals on a budget, save money or to learn the latest life hack!

Visit her Amazon Author Page to see her latest books:

amazon.com/author/laurasommers

Visit the Recipe Lady's blog for even more great recipes and to learn which books are **FREE** for download each week:

http://the-recipe-lady.blogspot.com/

Subscribe to The Recipe Lady blog through Amazon and have recipes and updates sent directly to your Kindle:

The Recipe Lady Blog through Amazon

Laura Sommers is also an Extreme Couponer and Penny Hauler! If you would like to find out how to get things for **FREE** with coupons or how to get things for only a **PENNY**, then visit her couponing blog **Penny Items and Freebies**

http://penny-items-and-freebies.blogspot.com/

Other books by Laura Sommers

- **Recipe Hacks for Saltine Crackers**
- **Recipe Hacks for Canned Biscuits**
- **Recipe Hacks for Canned Soup**
- **Recipe Hacks for Beer**
- **Recipe Hacks for Peanut Butter**
- **Recipe Hacks for Potato Chips**
- **Recipe Hacks for Oreo Cookies**
- **Recipe Hacks for Cheese Puffs**
- **Recipe Hacks for Pasta Sauce**
- **Recipe Hacks for Canned Tuna Fish**
- **Recipe Hacks for Dry Onion Soup Mix**
- **How to Shop for Penny Items**
- **Recipe Hacks for Dry Vegetable Soup Mix**

May all of your meals be a banquet
with good friends and good food.

Made in the USA
Las Vegas, NV
09 January 2023

65283157R00039